I0434636

Zelda's Rules

Zelda's Rules
A Self-Esteem Guide for Today's Black Woman

Harriet Thomas

Copyright © 2008 by Harriet Thomas

All rights reserved. No part of this book may be reproduced, stored, or transmitted by any means—whether auditory, graphic, mechanical, or electronic—without written permission of both publisher and author, except in the case of brief excerpts used in critical articles and reviews. Unauthorized reproduction of any part of this work is illegal and is punishable by law.

This book and the poems it contains are property of the Author. No Part of this book may be copied or distributed without the Author's permission.

Zelda's Rules: A Self-Esteem Guide for Today's Black Woman

ISBN 978-0-557-29603-3

Content ID 8264833

Acknowledgements

This book is written in loving memory of my mother. Harriet Taylor McMillon. She taught me to love myself and to be the best woman I can be. I can still feel her positive spiritual vibes although she is no longer with me in the flesh. I know she is smiling on me from heaven.

I love you Mama!

I would like to give honor and glory to God for with him all things are possible.

Thank you Isaiah my loving husband, for all your encouragement, support and patience. I love you!

To my children and grandchildren, Katrel, James, Adrian, Pam, Chris, Kiah, Malique, Shaun and B.J. - much love to you all - you are a blessing!

To my friends and the rest of my family - your support and good wishes mean the world to me. Thanks for believing in me.

I love you all!

Sisters - Conspire to Inspire!

We need to learn to communicate better so that we may grow and learn together. We are mothers, wives, sisters, aunts, daughters, friends, teachers, so many things.

We share a common bond - we are all divine females. The Path of the Divine Female is a journey into one's self, a discovery of the powers you hold as a woman. This is a journey towards empowerment and enlightenment and an ultimate acceptance of yourself and other women for who they truly are, not for what they look like or what they have.

Let the divine female in you encourage forgive, and love unconditionally.

So let's embark on this journey together, helping each other to learn and to grow to be the best we can be, giving honor, glory and thanks to our creator above.

I pray that the women who read this will receive it and be touched in some way.

May peace and love be upon you.

Zelda

Zelda's Rules

Chapter One - Rule #1

Love Yourself

How many times have you said or heard one of your single girlfriends say "I sure wish I could find a husband or "I need to find somebody who will love me for who I am and who will treat me with kindness and respect?" This is all well and good, but many times we don't even love and respect ourselves. We don't take the time to look in the mirror and really get to know who we are. We eat junk food; we don't exercise or get yearly checkups at the Dr. or the Dentist. Black women have a habit of trying to be everything to everybody and then neglect their own needs. They define "being strong" as being all things to all people, not taking any time for themselves. Some of us have these tremendous guilt feelings and will run ourselves into the ground before we will say "no" to those overbearing folks who are trying to sap the life's blood out of us. Then when we are lying in the street to weak to even move, we end up getting kicked to the curb by these same folks, on their way to claim their next victim!

Somebody should have told us! If we learn to love, respect and accept ourselves then we will not let this happen. We will feel empowered and will not let people make us feel guilty for saying "no". We will schedule some time just for ourselves every day, even if it's only 15 minutes to replenish and renew our spirit. Because let's face it ladies, dealing with men, children, needy family members, crazy co-workers and bosses on a daily basis can wear a sister out! If you don't do it now, start! You will feel better and be able to handle all of the trials and tribulations of everyday life without killing somebody!

Too many times I see a case where a woman has not gotten in touch with her deepest feelings to find out who she really is and what she really wants. What happens then is she meets someone when she is feeling lonely and unloved and she "settles" for a man who may have some issues of his own. These type men usually have addiction & job issues or baby mama drama and they typically prey on women who are lonely and looking for love. They can spot a woman who is feeling down and has low self-esteem from a mile away. I am convinced there is a special training camp for them where they learn how to do this. They will woo a woman and make her think that they are the best thing that has happened since the buy one get one half off sale at Payless Shoes! We fall into their trap, get involved with them and then later on in the relationship we wonder how in the hell did we end up with a no working, trifling, two timing fool we can't get rid of.

Learning to love accept, and value ourselves for who we are first, before we get into a relationship will give us a better chance of finding a man who will love, respect and value us also. When we think of ourselves as something wonderful and beautiful, something to be cherished, and conduct ourselves accordingly, then those positive vibes are put out into the universe for that special prince to pick up on. But if we go around with thoughts of low self worth, then we will attract the same kind of men.

These men don't even know how to be good to themselves; so how are they going to know how to treat a woman? God loves us and cherishes us just because we are. Let's honor and thank him for that by honoring ourselves.

So repeat after me:

"I promise to love, cherish and respect myself and I will only deal with men who will love, cherish and respect me and I won't settle for less"

"Show you're right"

Zelda

I AM A WOMAN

*I am as old as the mountains that rise majestically above the seas
& as wise as the owl that holds court in the trees.*

*I have borne life and mourned death. I have tasted the bitterness
of defeat and basked in the glow of victory.*

*I can be as gentle as a warm summer rain or as rough as the
winds of a tornado.*

*I have been torn down, only to rise up again that much stronger
and more determined.*

*I have been mistreated, misrepresented and mislead, but I have
endured.*

*My sisters are a myriad of colors and they stand with me as I
proclaim that I can, I shall and I will..Be all my creator meant me
to be...*
FOR I AM A WOMAN!!!
- Harriet Thomas-

Chapter Two - Rule #2

Smile Sister!!

Now this might be a touchy subject for some of you, but I have just got to put it out there. Why in the hell do some of us sisters go around looking like we are sucking on a sour lemon? I bet if we could see what we look like walking around with that "Damn it, I'll bite your or worse" look on our faces we might try to change our attitudes. Now I know everybody has some bad days and some of us are going through some rough times in our lives, but I have seen some sisters out in public looking so mean that I have crossed the street rather than walk on the same sidewalk with them! Now that is not good.

Ask yourself these questions. Is it so hard to smile? Is walking around looking like Medusa's sister going to make all your problems go away? When you see another sister would it kill you to smile and say "Hi"? Sisters we have got to learn to stop with the evilness towards one another. We will never grow as a person if we can't even give a smile to another human being. Besides I know you have heard the saying "It takes more muscles to frown than it does to smile."

So let's practice smiling instead of frowning. Smile at someone when they pass you by. The world is full of people who are hurting and your smile might be the only encouragement they get that day. Even if they don't smile back, it's ok because you are smiling because you feel good about yourself. Some people might look at you a little strangely, but hey at least they won't be breaking their neck trying to get away from your evil looking behind! Try it, I bet you will feel better and even if you don't feel better, you will sure in the hell look better - for real!!!

"Smile and the world will smile with you - frown and the birds will crap on your head"

"All right now"

Zelda

Sister My Sister

Sister my sister, can I talk with you for a minute? No, I don't want to hear your business cause I ain't trying to be in it.

I 'd just like to speak with you if I could and share my views on the lack of "real sisterhood".

You see I'm guilty and maybe you are the same of judging my sisters without even knowing their name. I look at their shape, comment on their hair and talk about what they really should or shouldn't wear.

I roll my big eyes, put my hands on my hips and not a kind word comes out of my "got the nerve" lips. Why can't I just smile, wave and say "Hey, I'm down with you sister, have a nice day"?

We need to stick together, it would be great if we could, to promote unity, understanding and "real" sisterhood. Without it we have nothing, why not go for it all? For sisters united we stand, divided we fall.

So let's seize the moment before the moment is gone. Grasp this message sister my sister and PASS IT ON! - Harriet Thomas –

Chapter Three - Rule #3

Girlfriends - Stop sitting around daydreaming about love

Do you remember when we were young and dreamed of growing up, falling in love and getting married to the most wonderful, handsome man in the world? We would play dress up and pretend that we were living this perfect, fairytale life. Come on now I know some of you remember wrapping yourself up in toilet paper; pretending to be a bride and your mother would have a hissy fit because you wasted all of that toilet paper! I know I got slapped upside the head more than once for wasting toilet paper - LOL!

Anyway, some of us are still looking for that "perfect fairytale romance" and it doesn't exist. Real life relationships take a lot of work. We have to learn to be patient and stop trying to live in a fairy tale world of love and romance. No prince is going to walk into the building you work in, pick you up and carry you off into the sunset. That only happens in the movies! Wake up and stop sitting there daydreaming at your desk. Some women have this idea of the perfect man in their head and while I am not saying we should just settle for anybody, some of us discount some good men as potential life mates because they don't fit a particular description, or they don't have the right kind of job or drive the right kind of car. Just because a man has a job making a six figure salary or drives a new Lexus does not mean that he is good boyfriend or husband material. I get so sick of hearing "Girl, he makes a lot of money " or "Girl, you should see his car". Now I am not saying that these are bad things but what about "Girl, he is so spiritual, he really treats me and others with kindness and respect". Or "He works hard and has the same values and beliefs as I do". We also tend to discount men right away because their physical appearance does not fit that idea of a "perfect man" that we have in our head. I am speaking from experience. I went through a terrible divorce and said I would never get married again. My first husband whom I thought was my dream man because he was the finest thing I had ever seen, turned out to be the husband from hell. I met the man who is now my husband of 16 years after my first marriage ended in divorce. Now I love my second husband with all my heart and I can truthfully say that after 16 years of marriage, we are more in love than ever; but when I first met him he did not fit the vision I had in my head in no way shape or form. My dream man was drop dead gorgeous. I mean he was Denzel Washington, Billy Dee Williams and the Rock all rolled up into one sexy, hot fudge sundae of a man with caramel sauce on the side. You know the kind of man who could walk p to you and say "Hi" and make you forget, who you are! Lord Have Mercy!

When I met my second husband I thought he looked ok, but I was not attracted to him at first. We talked and exchanged phone numbers and became friends over the course of 2 years. I dated other people, but found that he was very easy to talk to and I could confide in him without worrying about him judging me. We spent a lot of time together just hanging out. During our friendship I ended up getting engaged to this fine, tall, chocolate colored brother that I had only known for 3 months. This man had a good job making excellent money. His home and car were paid for. He spent $5,000 on an engagement ring for me and took me to the Bahamas. I was on cloud nine. He was nice and sweet and polite and got along well with my children, or so I thought. He got me to open up and talk about my dream man and he became everything I wanted, put an engagement ring on my finger and then all hell broke loose. Talk about a wolf in sheep's clothing, he was the wolf man! I found out why he was in such a hurry to get engaged. As soon as that ring was on my finger and I was "his property" his true self emerged. The man had a drinking problem and was mean and abusive when he got drunk. I was so anxious to find my dream man that I almost jumped out of the frying pan right into the damn fire! During this whole time the man (my second husband) who I had discounted because his looks were not up to my dream man standards was there for me. He helped me through that bad time and not once did he make a pass at me. He was patient and kind and whatever I needed him to be whenever I needed him to be it. I felt so safe and secure with him and as time passed I began to see the person he was inside and that person was my dream man! So ladies, let's take off the rose colored glasses when it comes to finding a mate..You might miss out on something good, looking for something that looks good!

"Everything that looks good is not necessarily good for you. Watch out for those fine wolves disguised as nice guys"

"Yea Buddy"

Zelda

Chapter Four - Rule #4

If it looks like crap and smells like crap-
It is Crap!!!

Now ladies - why, why, why do we always go and get into something that we know is not going to be good for us?

I mean all the signs will be there and we will still go on into it a leaping and a bounding and then when something goes wrong and I mean when, not if because we know that we know when we should leave someone or something along! Then when the crap hit's the fan we run to our girlfriends or our family crying talking about "Why did this happen to me"? Well it happened because you saw the crap and went ahead and stepped in it anyway and when it started to smell you wanted to get it off or your shoes.

What am I talking about here? I am talking about getting into relationships with men who we know from the get go are not good for us, but our stubborn behinds go on and let them in and they usually end up cleaning out our bank accounts, messing up our credit, tearing up our car, taking up residence in our house with no job, sleeping with our friends or worse becoming abusive to us and/or our children. The longer we have the crap in our lives the more it begins to stink. STAY AWAY FROM THE

CRAP! Crap has no redeeming qualities. You cannot change it into something that is desirable and smells good. Trust me, I have stepped in plenty of crap in my life and the deeper in it you step, the harder it is to get it off or your shoes.

If we learn to practice rule number one, which says we should love, honor and respect ourselves, then the crap doesn't have a snowball's chance in hell of getting anywhere near our shoes. It all starts with us loving and accepting ourselves. So when you come across a pile of crap, STOP! Don't sniff it, don't linger around it, just recognize it for what it is and do whatever you have to do to get away from it without stepping in it.

"I will not knowingly step in a pile of crap and if I find that I have indeed stepped in crap, I will immediately take action to get it the hell off of my shoes!!

" And you know that"

Zelda

A Free Woman
(What is a Free Woman?)

A free woman is someone who loves herself unconditionally, for she knows if she cannot love herself first, she will not be able to give unconditional love to another.

A free woman accepts herself from the tip of her toes to the top of her head. She knows she is a unique, one of a kind creation and is glorified with the knowledge that God does not make mistakes.

A free woman knows that she is beautiful in her own right. She realizes that true beauty comes from an inner, spiritual peace and a relationship with her creator, not from man made products.

A free woman does not base her opinion of herself on what others or society has to say. She is not defined by a mate, children, a career or material possessions, she realizes that these things enhance her life and considers them as a blessing.

A free woman does not gossip and is not jealous. She knows that these are negative traits and in order to be free she must live a positive life.

A Free woman does not compare herself to other women. Instead she embraces the diversity of all females and strives to keep an open mind so
That she might learn from those differences.
A free woman knows that she must learn to live by herself first and be comfortable before she can be comfortable in a relationship.

A free woman seeks a mate who will treat her with the love, respect and kindness she deserves and she in turn, will give the same to her mate.

A free woman takes care of her body for she realizes it is a temple and she treats it accordingly. She seeks those things that will feed her quest for spiritual knowledge and help her live a balanced life.

A free woman is not afraid to live her life as a tribute to her creator and she will fight to help those who are not yet free, break out of those chains that bind them, so that they too can fly to unimaginable heights........

Liberated...emancipated....unbound....FREE

- Harriet Thomas –

Chapter Five - Rule #5

Get Your Own Man

This is a subject that is near and dear to my heart. I know there are a lot of women out there who have had their hearts broken because their boyfriend/husband has cheated on them with another woman. This happened to me and it is part of the reason why I divorced my first husband. Not only did he cheat on me with someone who pretended to be my friend but he also had a baby with her while he was still married to me. Talk about ripping my heart out and doing the river dance on it! I was devastated. Why do women do this to each other? It's bad enough that some men don't seem to have a conscience when it comes to cheating, but what is even sadder is that there are women who think that dating a man who is supposed to be in a monogamous, committed relationship proves that they are somehow better than the other woman. Why? I have actually heard some women sit up and brag about dating a married man. Most of these women have been hurt in the past by a cheating mate and they figure what is good for the goose is good for the gander. They make up all sorts of excuses to try to convince themselves that there is a valid reason for messing around with someone else's man. But the bottom line is, there is no good, acceptable reason for a woman to knowingly sleep with some other woman's husband or mate. I don't care how you choose to look at it. Ladies, those of you who have been hurt, just stop and think a moment how bad it made you feel. For most of us it is a horrible feeling. So if we remember how bad this made us feel when it was done to us, why would we want to inflict that hurt on another sister? Now some people would say, well it's just as much the man's fault, and the men know they are attached and that may be true, but that doesn't mean you have to go along with his game if you find out he is in a committed relationship. I know that some men lie about being in committed relationships and you do not find out until after you have done the horizontal mambo that he is married or attached. But that still doesn't make it ok to keep on seeing him. If you find out that he lied to you, take steps to end the relationship right away. Think about it; do you really want to begin a relationship with someone who has lied to you right from the start? The longer you put it off, the harder it is to break it off., It truly saddens me when I see someone I know male or female out in public with another person's spouse or mate acting like everything is just hunky dory. It makes me want to run over and tattoo a big A right on their foreheads. Imagine what would happen if every woman made a solemn vow NOT to engage in any relationship with men who are in a committed relationship with another woman. Now wouldn't that be something? Men would be running around here losing their damn minds! As wonderful as that sounds, I realize that it's probably asking too much. But remember, change always starts with one person and if we are at a place where we respect and love ourselves then we won't even think about sleeping with someone else's man. Do we really want to be number two? Because that is what we are when we get into a relationship with a man who is already married or in a committed relationship. Ladies let's learn to respect ourselves enough not to "settle" for being someone's second choice. Why be potato salad when you are worthy of being a prime cut of steak?

Come on Ladies - say it for me now:

I will not knowingly sleep with another woman's husband or mate. I will not be a side dish because I am worthy of being the choice main course"

"Go Ladies - Go Ladies"

Zelda

The Essence of a Black Woman

THE ESSENCE OF A BLACK WOMAN IS A WONDER TO BEHOLD

Energy emanates from deep inside her soul and creates an aura of mystery - to complex to be fully explained.

The glory of her multi-sepia hues are often imitated, but never duplicated. Chocolate pecan, peanut butter, mocha, café' au lait, black licorice, hazelnut cream - a veritable buffet of rich colors, each one beautiful in its own right.

Her crowning glory is a testament to her multifaceted personalities - Cultural, trendy, sassy, sexy, sophisticated and she wears them all with the pride that was instilled by her ancestors hundreds of years ago.

She has a regal bearing, for she is a Queen. No matter what her occupation may be, she handles her business with a flair that only she can bring - a style that is all her own.

The essence of her beauty is exotic and timeless. Nubian inspired beauty flows through her veins and shines on her face like a multitude of stars twinkling in the midnight sky.

She is mother earth, the color of soil - the goddess of the universe.

She can cook a meal that will make the taste buds in your mouth stand at attention with anticipation. She can enfold you in her arms and make everything all right.

She loves passionately, faithfully and completely, leaving her man wanting for nothing but more of her sweet Georgia brown self.

The essence of a black woman is a gift from our Heavenly Father. Her struggles have not gone unnoticed. By the grace of God she was able to rise from the ashes like the mythical phoenix and her graceful flight is just beginning.

So go forth my sisters and let your essence shine for all the world to see. For the essence of a black woman is a precious gift.

Receive it and be blessed!
- Harriet Thomas-

Chapter Six - Rule #6

Physical and Mental Abuse

Ok girlfriends, I want you to listen and listen good, as a matter of fact I want you to repeat the following words out loud. Look in the mirror and say "PHYSICAL AND MENTAL ABUSE HAVE NO PLACE IN A RELATIONSHIP!!! If you are in a relationship where your mate has been abusive to you whether it is verbally, mentally or lord forbid, physically you are traveling down a very dangerous road. So many of us tend to ignore the warning signs and end up getting hurt very badly or even killed. We hear sad stories everyday about women being killed or disabled because they stayed in an abusive relationship. Why do we stay? We are really fooling ourselves if we think that they will never hit us again, or that we can change them. Men who abuse women generally have deep rooted issues that you can do nothing about. In other words their butts need some serious therapy! We need to quit trying to play Dr. Phil and stop making excuses for them.

Like "Oh I made him mad, I know better, it was all my fault". If he hits you upside your head just because you made him mad, the man has issues. Most of them will apologize and feel guilty afterwards. They cry, beg your forgiveness and tell you that it will never happen again. But eight times out of ten, it does happen again and again and again. In most cases the abuse gets worse and happens more frequently and we as women lose a little bit more of our soul and many times end up being a shell of the person we once were. We blame ourselves and do everything we can to feel "worthy" in his eyes. But the problem is we will never be good enough, thin enough, pretty enough, or just plain enough of anything because most abusive men have self-esteem issues and they don't feel worthy, which makes them mad so they direct their anger at you. Again, I am speaking from experience. I was in an abusive relationship for years and it went from bad to worse to good for a while to downright terrible. The first time he hit me I was so shocked that to this day it is hard for me to believe that the wonderful, caring man I thought I knew and wanted to marry one day had behaved like that. After the first time he hit me, it continued and got progressively worse. He would cry and say he was sorry and beg my forgiveness. I wanted to believe that he loved me as much as I loved him and I had convinced myself that it was my fault that he hit me. So I stayed and fooled myself into thinking that things would get better and eventually they did for a while; which is why I ended up marrying him and it was one of the biggest mistakes of my life. I naively thought that marriage would magically change him and the abuse would stop after we were married. Instead the abuse continued with a vengeance and I felt like I was living in a nightmare. I was ashamed and scared to leave at the same time. Then I convinced myself that I was staying for my children, but that too was a mistake. Children know more than we give them credit for and all the things I thought I was hiding from them, they knew and it affected them both very deeply. My husband even came to my job one day and threatened me at my desk. After that I had no choice, so I got up the courage to leave him and filed for a divorce. But the abuse did not stop there. He continued to threaten me and followed me everywhere. He even tried to get me thrown out of the apartment I had rented after I left him. I was a nervous wreck. I ended up having to get a restraining order to keep him away from me and even that didn't work at times. I had to be mindful when I was leaving my apartment to go anywhere, never knowing when he was just going to show up.

There were so many signs early in our relationship pointing to the fact that he needed help, but I chose to ignore them because I thought I was in love and my children and I paid dearly for that. So ladies remember, if your husband or boyfriend is jealous, hits you or says demeaning things to you one minute and then turns around and tells you he loves you the next, something is not right. Love does not hit, demean, threaten, force, punch, kick, slap or control. If you are in a relationship where someone does any of these things to you and tells you it is love, they are telling a lie. They need help and if you stay then you do too. You can't fix something that doesn't even know it's broken. Love yourself girlfriends. I can't stress that enough because if you love yourself you will not let anyone abuse you, no way, no how.

"I deserve to be treated with kindness and respect. I do not have time for any man who feels the need to abuse me in any way. If I find myself in an abusive relationship, I need to lace up my Nikes and run."

"On the serious tip"

Zelda

A Strong Black Woman

Hey Brother, Yes I'm talking to you my fine chocolate warrior. Don't take my kindness for weakness - For I am a strong Black Woman.

Yes, I love you, I even adore you. I don't mind cooking your dinner or washing your clothes as long as you remember to treat me like the Black Queen that I am. Love me, respect me, comfort me, protect me. If you can't do that, leave me be, because I won't settle for less - For I am a strong Black Woman.

I will raise my children on my own, if I have to. Work, pay my own bills and put food on the table. But don't misunderstand me, I am not saying I don't need you, I do. But I don't need your disrespect, your abuse or your unfaithfulness. I deserve the best and I won't settle for less - For I am a strong Black Woman.

I will stand by your side and help to ease your burdens. I will be there with open arms and a soft warm body to comfort you. But don't take my softness for weakness, because I will not be your escape goat, your whipping post or your doormat. - For I am a strong Black Woman.

I will pray with you, lay with you, bear your children, make your house a home and treat you like the Black Prince that you are. All I ask is that you treat me the way I know I deserve to be treated. If you can't do that, then leave me alone and I will be ok because I know there is someone out there who will cherish me. I deserve the best and I won't settle for less - For I am a strong Black Woman.

-Harriet Thomas-

Chapter Seven - Rule#7

Relationships

How many of you have ever been in a relationship where you thought everything was going great. You both were employed, had joint ownership of material possessions and had been together for quite a while and in your mind you thought that the next logical step you two were going to take would be to the altar? You mentally started planning your wedding, your dress, your cake, what your bridesmaids would wear. Your birthday was coming up and you just knew you were getting an engagement ring and then when you opened your gift and saw it was indeed a piece of jewelry but not the piece of jewelry you were looking for, you smiled and said "thank you" and convinced yourself that he was waiting to surprise you at Christmas. Christmas came and went and the third finger on your left hand was sprung because you were secretly practicing sticking it up in your girlfriends faces to show them the 31/2 carat, princess cut diamond ring you just knew you were going to get, but it never appeared. Your girlfriends got married and you were a bridesmaid but never a bride. You found yourself starting to drop all kinds of hints, but your man did not seem to get it. So you charged $75.00 on your credit card to call Ms. Cleo to see if she could predict when he was going to pop the question. You even called your cousin down in Louisiana and asked her to send you some love potion and you fed it to your man for three weeks straight and he still did not propose. By this time you are feeling quite desperate and you start threatening to leave, even though you don't really mean it. Then horror of all horrors you actually try to get pregnant on purpose thinking that if you have his baby he will marry you. Most of the time when a woman does that, all she ends up with is a baby that she has to raise all by herself - an unwed mother instead of a bride. Ladies all of this can be avoided if we make sure our man is on the same page we are before we get into a serious relationship with him. We need to stop using sex as a way to get or keep a man. Our bodies are precious and we need to remember that. So many of us are in such a hurry to have a relationship or "have a man" that we don't bother to discuss important details and really get to know him before we become sexually and seriously involved with him. We need to ask questions like - how does he feel about marriage? Does he already have children and if he does, does he help support and raise them? Would he like any more children? If you have children is he a good father/role model? What kind of relationship does he have with his mother or his sisters? Does he believe in the sanctity of marriage or does he think it is ok to live together for 49 years? Is he even husband material?

If the man is not on the same page we are, we can drop hints until the cows come home and he still will not get it. Trust me on this one! I lived with a man for 10 years and had two kids by him and he still did not want to marry me. He only married me because of pressure from his family. Not only was he not on the same page I was on when it came to marriage and family values, he was reading out of an entirely different book, one that I had never heard of. Bottom line is that you BOTH have to be committed to the same goal. If your goal is to get married and his is to live together, yall are going to have some serious issues. I learned the hard way that you shouldn't have to make anybody marry you and when you really think about it, why would you want to? Take your time and find out what book your man is reading before you join his book club.

"I will take my time and find out what kind of book the man is reading before I get too serious and find out that I am reading "Brides" magazine and he is reading "Living Single"

"You know damn right"

Zelda

Chapter Eight - Rule#8

Stop Comparing Yourself to Other Women!!!

How many times have you been somewhere, a party or another public function and notice a woman come in who is dressed perfectly from her head to her toes? I mean a sister who really had it going on and was beautiful on top of it. Did you stand there and look her up and down with a "Who does she think she is" expression? Did you say to yourself, "She must have money, I could look like that if I had her money" or some other less than flattering comment. Come on now, be honest, I know I have done it a few times in my life, but that was before I learned to love myself and be happy with who I am.

We women have a bad habit of looking at what other females have and comparing ourselves to them and when we do that we always seem to come up short. We find ourselves questioning why we cannot have the same kind of house, car, relationship, job, body, hair and so on, the list is endless. Some of us even go so far as to place ourselves in some serious debt just to prove to ourselves that we can have what they have. The problem with this is that we really don't know what is going on in other people's lives. We don't know what those other females have sacrificed or are sacrificing to have what they have. We are so busy worrying about what they have that we don't even stop to think that maybe they worked really hard to get what they have and are working hard to keep it. In other words they are tending to their own business and we should take a hint from them and tend to ours. We are just on the outside looking in, we convince ourselves that if we had a husband or mate or home or job like another female that we would be happy. Things are not always as they seem and too many of us put so much emphasis on material things or looks or money and feel we are "lacking" something in our lives because we don't have those things. Material things can be lost in a split second.. Remember ladies."The grass may look greener on the other side of the fence, but sooner or later someone is going to have to mow it." So tend to your own lawn, if you water, feed and give it what it needs to grow you will have a beautiful lawn. However, if you spend your time looking over the fence at someone else's lawn, yours is going to die from neglect.

"I will work on myself from the inside out, to be the best I can be and make an effort not to compare myself to other women."

"Handle your business"

Zelda

SUCH AS I AM

Such as I am in a manner of speaking..
Jutting lips, big behind, rounded hips - one of a kind.

Such as I am in a manner of speaking
Chocolate brown, butter light, pecan sandy, black as night.

Such as I am in a manner of speaking
Straight, natural, curly hair
My crowning glory shows cultural flair.

Such as I am in a manner of speaking
Still standing tall after 300 years of
Hatred, injustice, blood sweat and tears.

Proud regal bearing..Reigning supreme
Such as I am
An African Queen.
-Harriet Thomas-

Chapter Nine - Rule #9

Dress Appropriately - Please!

Now here is another subject that is touchy and may offend a few ladies, but I would be remiss if I didn't say something about it in this book. Ladies, why is it that a lot of us insist on wearing clothing that is meant for someone 10, 20 or lord forbid 30 years younger than us? Or, clothing that is too tight, too short, too revealing for our body type and weight? I have seen outfits on some women that made me wonder how in the heck they even got in them. Did they look in the mirror before they left the house? Who told them that looking like a mattress with a string tied around it was sexy? Just because spandex stretches doesn't mean it was meant for anyone with any body shape. On the other hand I have seen women with very nice shapes in some of the most hideous, stripper/call girl looking outfits that defy everything decent. When we wear inappropriate clothing we send the wrong messages and the wrong men are always the ones who pick up on those messages. There are a lot of men out there who feel that women who dress in extremely revealing clothing are just asking to be talked to in a disrespectful manner, called names or worse groped or attacked. Not saying this is right, but its unfortunately true and we need to be aware that if we dress in revealing clothing, we could be inviting trouble. To the rest of the world we just look like a fool who refused to acknowledge the fact that we look ridiculous in the clothing we are wearing. We all can't be a size six and truth be told there are more size tens, twelve's and fourteens out there anyway. The most important thing is that we are healthy and we like ourselves and if we want to lose weight and get in shape, we do it for the right reason, not because society, fashion magazines and music videos suggest that we as females have to look like broomsticks or dress like strippers to be desirable. We can be sexy at any size. There are so many new and different clothing styles on the market today for women of all shapes and sizes. We also have to remember that revealing to the point of damn near being naked does not mean "sexy". Now if you want to put on some stripper shoes, a see through top and a thong and parade around the house with the shades down, that's a different story. But don't bring your butt outside going to the grocery store in that mess and have the nerve to get mad when someone looks at you the wrong way.

If you are going to go around dressed like that, you might as well go to work in a strip club and get paid for it! Bottom line ladies, be proud of who you are and what you look like no matter what size or shape you are and when you are comfortable with who you are and what you look like, you will dress in age appropriate, size appropriate, tasteful clothing and I won't have to call the fashion police on you!

Come on Ladies, you know the drill, repeat after me:

"I will dress in clothing that fits my age, body style and size and I will not come out of the house dressed like Lil Kim's sister."

"Bad girls, Bad girls, what cha gonna do?"
Zelda

Black Woman
You've Got Style

From that glide in your stride to that zip in your hips, those mysterious eyes and your full pouting lips..Black Woman-You've got style!
You're a full spectrum of colors from mocha to cream, your beauty is timeless and your reign supreme..Black Woman-You've got style!
You're strong, yet gentle, you're statuesque and proud. Your essence is regal and you stand out in a crowd, Black Woman-You've got style!
You're intelligent & sexy, you're feminine, yet tough, you've got it all together and you know you're stuff..Black Woman-You've got style!

You're the mother of a nation, a ruler of the earth, no jewels,
gold or silver could compare to your worth..Black Woman-
You've got style!
You make all the homeboys want to stay awhile when you walk
down the street and give them that smile..Black Woman - You've
got Style!

- Harriet Thomas-

Chapter Ten - Rule #10

Get in touch with your Spiritual Self

This is the most important rule of all, so ladies pay close attention. If we want to live a positive, peaceful and happy life, we must get in touch with our inner spiritual selves. Once we learn to tap into that inner strength that we were all born with, we will look at life from a different perspective. Now, I m not saying that we will no longer have problems, but we will have gained a new insight and this will enable us to handle our problems in a different manner.

Things that used to seem impossible and insurmountable will become possible and smaller. We will be more at peace with ourselves and also with others. We will learn to stop taking things that people say and do as a personal attack and we will be able to accept those things that we can't do anything about. We will understand that "we can't change people' but we can change how we react to them. We will be able to "let go and let God." We will pray when things get tough and pray when things are going great. We will learn to turn a deaf ear to gossip and rumors because this is destructive, hurtful behavior and we will no longer feel the need to be a part of such negative things.

When we put on our spiritual armor all the arrows and spears that are thrown at us will be deflected and fall at our feet and we will step over them and pray for those who dared to shoot them at us.

We will learn to be more tolerant, have more compassion and be less judgmental.

The more we get to know our inner spiritual selves, the happier, peaceful and loving we will become. We will love ourselves unconditionally and in turn will be able to give unconditional love to others. This goes back to the first rule; LOVE YOURSELF. When you love yourself, you are ultimately loving our creator, for he lives in us all, he is just waiting for us to acknowledge him.

"I will get in touch with my inner, spiritual self and practice seeking love, joy and peace on a daily basis"

"Amen"

Zelda

I AM SOMEBODY

I am somebody…
I am a beautiful flower in a field of many
Each perfect petal created by the loving hands
Of my Heavenly Father.

I am a rainbow of vibrant colors
Each one unique in brightness and intensity
But special just the same.

I m a mountain standing tall and proud
With snow capped peaks, offering up
A silent prayer to the sky.

I am a river, flowing free and pure
Into the never ending ocean of life.

I am one of a kind

I am a miracle

I am a living testimony to the magnificence
Of God's love and grace.

I AM SOMEBODY

- Harriet Thomas-

This book is dedicated to all my sisters.

My mission is to inspire, to let you know that you are beautiful and worthy. You are a divine female. When you understand how special you are, I hope that you will pass it on. We owe it to each other to uplift and encourage.

I have included some journal pages at the end of this book. Please take the time to write down at least one positive thought a day. It is a great way to keep your mind on a positive track. Go out into the world and let your light shine!

May God bless you!

Harriet Thomas AKA "Zelda'

Journal of Positive Thoughts

"I can do all things through Christ who strengthens me"
Philippians 4:13

Name: _____

*Date:*_____

Today I am thankful for:

_____
_____
_____
_____
_____
_____

Positive thought:

_____
_____
_____
_____
_____
_____
_____
_____
_____
_____
_____
_____
_____
_____
_____
_____
_____
_____
_____

*Date:*_____

Today I am thankful for:

_____
_____
_____
_____
_____
_____

Positive thought:

_____
_____
_____
_____
_____
_____
_____
_____
_____
_____
_____
_____
_____
_____
_____
_____
_____
_____
_____
_____

*Date:*_____

Today I am thankful for:

_____
_____
_____
_____
_____
_____

Positive thought:

_____
_____
_____
_____
_____
_____
_____
_____
_____
_____
_____
_____
_____
_____
_____
_____
_____
_____
_____
_____
_____

*Date:*_____

Today I am thankful for:

_____
_____
_____
_____
_____
_____

Positive thought:

_____
_____
_____
_____
_____
_____
_____
_____
_____
_____
_____
_____
_____
_____
_____
_____
_____
_____
_____
_____
_____

*Date:*_____

Today I am thankful for:

_____
_____
_____
_____
_____
_____

Positive thought:

_____
_____
_____
_____
_____
_____
_____
_____
_____
_____
_____
_____
_____
_____
_____
_____
_____
_____
_____
_____

*Date:*_____

Today I am thankful for:

_____
_____
_____
_____
_____
_____

Positive thought:

_____
_____
_____
_____
_____
_____
_____
_____
_____
_____
_____
_____
_____
_____
_____
_____
_____
_____
_____
_____
_____
_____

*Date:*_____

Today I am thankful for:

_____
_____
_____
_____
_____
_____

Positive thought:

_____
_____
_____
_____
_____
_____
_____
_____
_____
_____
_____
_____
_____
_____
_____
_____
_____
_____
_____
_____

*Date:*_____

Today I am thankful for:

_____
_____
_____
_____
_____
_____

Positive thought:

_____
_____
_____
_____
_____
_____
_____
_____
_____
_____
_____
_____
_____
_____
_____
_____
_____
_____
_____
_____

*Date:*_____

Today I am thankful for:

_____
_____
_____
_____
_____
_____

Positive thought:

_____
_____
_____
_____
_____
_____
_____
_____
_____
_____
_____
_____
_____
_____
_____
_____
_____
_____
_____
_____
_____

*Date:*_____

Today I am thankful for:

_____
_____
_____
_____
_____
_____

Positive thought:

_____
_____
_____
_____
_____
_____
_____
_____
_____
_____
_____
_____
_____
_____
_____
_____
_____
_____

Date:_____

Today I am thankful for:

_____
_____
_____
_____
_____
_____

Positive thought:

_____
_____
_____
_____
_____
_____
_____
_____
_____
_____
_____
_____
_____
_____
_____
_____
_____
_____
_____
_____
_____

*Date:*_____

Today I am thankful for:

_____
_____
_____
_____
_____
_____

Positive thought:

_____
_____
_____
_____
_____
_____
_____
_____
_____
_____
_____
_____
_____
_____
_____
_____
_____
_____
_____

*Date:*_____

Today I am thankful for:

_____
_____
_____
_____
_____
_____

Positive thought:

_____
_____
_____
_____
_____
_____
_____
_____
_____
_____
_____
_____
_____
_____
_____
_____
_____
_____
_____
_____
_____

*Date:*_____

Today I am thankful for:

_____
_____
_____
_____
_____
_____

Positive thought:

_____
_____
_____
_____
_____
_____
_____
_____
_____
_____
_____
_____
_____
_____
_____
_____
_____
_____
_____
_____

*Date:*_____

Today I am thankful for:

_____
_____
_____
_____
_____
_____

Positive thought:

_____
_____
_____
_____
_____
_____
_____
_____
_____
_____
_____
_____
_____
_____
_____
_____
_____
_____
_____
_____

*Date:*_____

Today I am thankful for:

_____
_____
_____
_____
_____
_____

Positive thought:

_____
_____
_____
_____
_____
_____
_____
_____
_____
_____
_____
_____
_____
_____
_____
_____
_____
_____
_____
_____

Date:_____

Today I am thankful for:

_____
_____
_____
_____
_____
_____

Positive thought:

_____
_____
_____
_____
_____
_____
_____
_____
_____
_____
_____
_____
_____
_____
_____
_____
_____
_____
_____

*Date:*_____

Today I am thankful for:

_____
_____
_____
_____
_____
_____

Positive thought:

_____
_____
_____
_____
_____
_____
_____
_____
_____
_____
_____
_____
_____
_____
_____
_____
_____
_____
_____

*Date:*_____

Today I am thankful for:

_____
_____
_____
_____
_____
_____

Positive thought:

_____
_____
_____
_____
_____
_____
_____
_____
_____
_____
_____
_____
_____
_____
_____
_____
_____
_____
_____

*Date:*_____

Today I am thankful for:

_____
_____
_____
_____
_____
_____

Positive thought:

_____
_____
_____
_____
_____
_____
_____
_____
_____
_____
_____
_____
_____
_____
_____
_____
_____
_____
_____

*Date:*_____

Today I am thankful for:

_____
_____
_____
_____
_____
_____

Positive thought:

_____
_____
_____
_____
_____
_____
_____
_____
_____
_____
_____
_____
_____
_____
_____
_____
_____
_____
_____

*Date:*_____

Today I am thankful for:

_____
_____
_____
_____
_____
_____

Positive thought:

_____
_____
_____
_____
_____
_____
_____
_____
_____
_____
_____
_____
_____
_____
_____
_____
_____
_____
_____
_____

*Date:*_____

Today I am thankful for:

_____
_____
_____
_____
_____
_____

Positive thought:

_____
_____
_____
_____
_____
_____
_____
_____
_____
_____
_____
_____
_____
_____
_____
_____
_____
_____
_____
_____

*Date:*_____

Today I am thankful for:

_____
_____
_____
_____
_____
_____

Positive thought:

_____
_____
_____
_____
_____
_____
_____
_____
_____
_____
_____
_____
_____
_____
_____
_____
_____
_____
_____

*Date:*_____

Today I am thankful for:

_____
_____
_____
_____
_____
_____

Positive thought:

_____
_____
_____
_____
_____
_____
_____
_____
_____
_____
_____
_____
_____
_____
_____
_____
_____
_____
_____
_____

*Date:*_____

Today I am thankful for:

_____
_____
_____
_____
_____
_____

Positive thought:

_____
_____
_____
_____
_____
_____
_____
_____
_____
_____
_____
_____
_____
_____
_____
_____
_____
_____
_____

*Date:*_____

Today I am thankful for:

_____
_____
_____
_____
_____
_____

Positive thought:

_____
_____
_____
_____
_____
_____
_____
_____
_____
_____
_____
_____
_____
_____
_____
_____
_____
_____
_____

*Date:*_____

Today I am thankful for:

_____
_____
_____
_____
_____
_____

Positive thought:

_____
_____
_____
_____
_____
_____
_____
_____
_____
_____
_____
_____
_____
_____
_____
_____
_____
_____
_____

*Date:*_____

Today I am thankful for:

_____
_____
_____
_____
_____
_____

Positive thought:

_____
_____
_____
_____
_____
_____
_____
_____
_____
_____
_____
_____
_____
_____
_____
_____
_____
_____
_____
_____
_____

*Date:*_____

Today I am thankful for:

_____
_____
_____
_____
_____
_____

Positive thought:

_____
_____
_____
_____
_____
_____
_____
_____
_____
_____
_____
_____
_____
_____
_____
_____
_____
_____
_____

*Date:*_____

Today I am thankful for:

_____
_____
_____
_____
_____
_____

Positive thought:

_____
_____
_____
_____
_____
_____
_____
_____
_____
_____
_____
_____
_____
_____
_____
_____
_____
_____
_____
_____

*Date:*_____

Today I am thankful for:

_____
_____
_____
_____
_____
_____

Positive thought:

_____
_____
_____
_____
_____
_____
_____
_____
_____
_____
_____
_____
_____
_____
_____
_____
_____
_____
_____

*Date:*_____

Today I am thankful for:

_____
_____
_____
_____
_____
_____

Positive thought:

_____
_____
_____
_____
_____
_____
_____
_____
_____
_____
_____
_____
_____
_____
_____
_____
_____
_____
_____

*Date:*_____

Today I am thankful for:

_____
_____
_____
_____
_____
_____

Positive thought:

_____
_____
_____
_____
_____
_____
_____
_____
_____
_____
_____
_____
_____
_____
_____
_____
_____
_____
_____
_____

*Date:*_____

Today I am thankful for:

_____
_____
_____
_____
_____
_____

Positive thought:

_____
_____
_____
_____
_____
_____
_____
_____
_____
_____
_____
_____
_____
_____
_____
_____
_____
_____
_____
_____
_____
_____

*Date:*_____

Today I am thankful for:

_____
_____
_____
_____
_____
_____

Positive thought:

_____
_____
_____
_____
_____
_____
_____
_____
_____
_____
_____
_____
_____
_____
_____
_____
_____
_____
_____
_____
_____
_____
_____

*Date:*_____

Today I am thankful for:

_____
_____
_____
_____
_____
_____

Positive thought:

_____
_____
_____
_____
_____
_____
_____
_____
_____
_____
_____
_____
_____
_____
_____
_____
_____
_____
_____
_____
_____

*Date:*_____

Today I am thankful for:

_____
_____
_____
_____
_____
_____

Positive thought:

_____
_____
_____
_____
_____
_____
_____
_____
_____
_____
_____
_____
_____
_____
_____
_____
_____
_____
_____
_____
_____
_____

*Date:*_____

Today I am thankful for:

_____
_____
_____
_____
_____
_____

Positive thought:

_____
_____
_____
_____
_____
_____
_____
_____
_____
_____
_____
_____
_____
_____
_____
_____
_____
_____
_____

*Date:*_____

Today I am thankful for:

_____
_____
_____
_____
_____
_____

Positive thought:

_____
_____
_____
_____
_____
_____
_____
_____
_____
_____
_____
_____
_____
_____
_____
_____
_____
_____
_____
_____

*Date:*_____

Today I am thankful for:

_____
_____
_____
_____
_____
_____

Positive thought:

_____
_____
_____
_____
_____
_____
_____
_____
_____
_____
_____
_____
_____
_____
_____
_____
_____
_____
_____
_____
_____

*Date:*_____

Today I am thankful for:

_____
_____
_____
_____
_____
_____

Positive thought:

_____
_____
_____
_____
_____
_____
_____
_____
_____
_____
_____
_____
_____
_____
_____
_____
_____
_____
_____
_____

*Date:*_____

Today I am thankful for:

_____
_____
_____
_____
_____
_____

Positive thought:

_____
_____
_____
_____
_____
_____
_____
_____
_____
_____
_____
_____
_____
_____
_____
_____
_____
_____
_____
_____

*Date:*_____

Today I am thankful for:

_____
_____
_____
_____
_____
_____

Positive thought:

_____
_____
_____
_____
_____
_____
_____
_____
_____
_____
_____
_____
_____
_____
_____
_____
_____
_____
_____
_____
_____

*Date:*_____

Today I am thankful for:

_____
_____
_____
_____
_____
_____

Positive thought:

_____
_____
_____
_____
_____
_____
_____
_____
_____
_____
_____
_____
_____
_____
_____
_____
_____
_____
_____
_____

*Date:*_____

Today I am thankful for:

_____
_____
_____
_____
_____
_____

Positive thought:

_____
_____
_____
_____
_____
_____
_____
_____
_____
_____
_____
_____
_____
_____
_____
_____
_____
_____
_____
_____
_____

*Date:*_____

Today I am thankful for:

_____
_____
_____
_____
_____
_____

Positive thought:

_____
_____
_____
_____
_____
_____
_____
_____
_____
_____
_____
_____
_____
_____
_____
_____
_____
_____
_____

*Date:*_____

Today I am thankful for:

_____
_____
_____
_____
_____
_____

Positive thought:

_____
_____
_____
_____
_____
_____
_____
_____
_____
_____
_____
_____
_____
_____
_____
_____
_____
_____
_____
_____

*Date:*_____

Today I am thankful for:

_____
_____
_____
_____
_____
_____

Positive thought:

_____
_____
_____
_____
_____
_____
_____
_____
_____
_____
_____
_____
_____
_____
_____
_____
_____
_____
_____
_____
_____
_____

*Date:*_____

Today I am thankful for:

_____
_____
_____
_____
_____
_____

Positive thought:

_____
_____
_____
_____
_____
_____
_____
_____
_____
_____
_____
_____
_____
_____
_____
_____
_____
_____
_____
_____

*Date:*_____

Today I am thankful for:

_____
_____
_____
_____
_____
_____

Positive thought:

_____
_____
_____
_____
_____
_____
_____
_____
_____
_____
_____
_____
_____
_____
_____
_____
_____
_____
_____
_____

*Date:*_____

Today I am thankful for:

_____
_____
_____
_____
_____
_____

Positive thought:

_____
_____
_____
_____
_____
_____
_____
_____
_____
_____
_____
_____
_____
_____
_____
_____
_____
_____
_____
_____
_____

*Date:*_____

Today I am thankful for:

_____
_____
_____
_____
_____
_____

Positive thought:

_____
_____
_____
_____
_____
_____
_____
_____
_____
_____
_____
_____
_____
_____
_____
_____
_____
_____
_____
_____

*Date:*_____

Today I am thankful for:

_____
_____
_____
_____
_____
_____

Positive thought:

_____
_____
_____
_____
_____
_____
_____
_____
_____
_____
_____
_____
_____
_____
_____
_____
_____
_____
_____
_____
_____

www.ingramcontent.com/pod-product-compliance
Lightning Source LLC
Chambersburg PA
CBHW020310290526
45784CB00003B/1447